Crossing a bridge requires trust that the structure is sturdy, reliable, and will be there to support you as you go about your business.

Nauticom.net

How to Lead From a Distance

Building Bridges in the Virtual Workplace

Debra A. Dinnocenzo

The WALK ·THE· TALK® Company

Helping organizations achieve success through Ethical
Leadership and Values-Based Business Practices

How to Lead From a Distance

Inquiries regarding permission for use of the material contained in this book should be addressed to:
The WALK THE TALK Company
2925 LBJ Freeway, Suite 201
Dallas, Texas 75234
972.243.8863

WALK THE TALK books may be purchased for educational, business, or sales promotion use.

WALK THE TALK® and The WALK THE TALK® Company are registered trademarks of
Performance Systems Corporation.

Printed in the United States of America
10 9 8 7 6 5 4 3 2 1

Edited by Michelle Sedas
Designed and Printed by Branch-Smith

ISBN 1-885228-73-2

HOW TO LEAD FROM A DISTANCE

Building Bridges in the Virtual Workplace

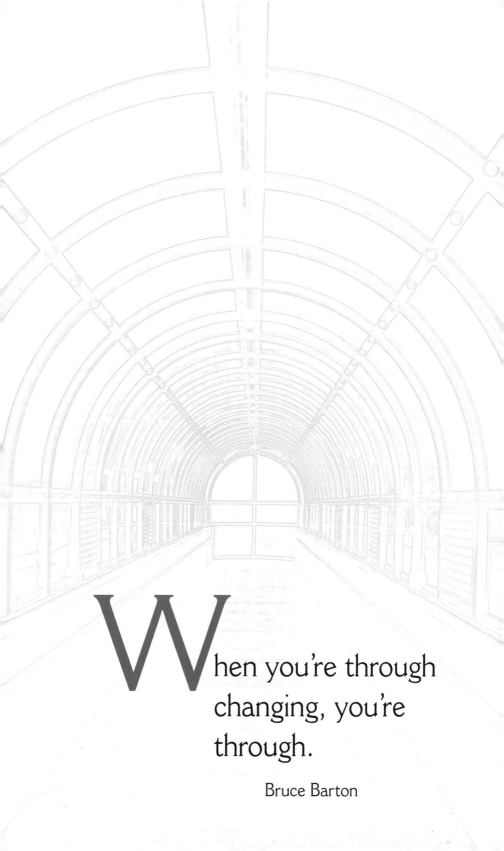

When you're through changing, you're through.

Bruce Barton

INTRODUCTION

The days of going to work and seeing everyone you work with are gone forever!

The ways we "see" one another, communicate, build teams, establish trust, collaborate, and achieve results have all changed. Separation brings a whole new set of issues and problems. And leaders must adapt by bridging the gaps that can occur when people work apart from one another.

What was once a nontraditional way of working is now commonplace. Managing from a distance is a growing reality for leaders across a broad spectrum of organizations and industries. So if this describes you, your team, your organization – or how it could become where you work – you need to prepare, as a leader, to build bridges across the virtual workplace.

Look around – there are signs everywhere of the need to change with changing times and ways of leading. Increases in mergers, expanding global operations, decreased travel budgets, and worker demands are propelling many organizations into geographically dispersed environments. And this means you need to build bridges — and close gaps — to connect people in the virtual world. The three key bridges you must build are:

❖ *Trust*
❖ *Communication*
❖ *Performance*

This book will show you how to do that — as you explore what's different (and what isn't) about leading in a virtual work environment. Many of your existing management and leadership skills are still important — but not sufficient for the leadership demands of the virtual workplace. That's about to change!

The skills to lead virtually are needed for many different situations. Whether you're responsible for a small team with some or all members remote or you manage a large group with multiple teams operating at various levels of remote work, you're leading from a distance. In a nutshell, you must now "talk" with people, motivate and coach, provide feedback, and offer support — all without the "comfort zone" of face-to-face communication. Learning how to "connect" with people remotely and get results from a distance is your key to virtual leadership success.

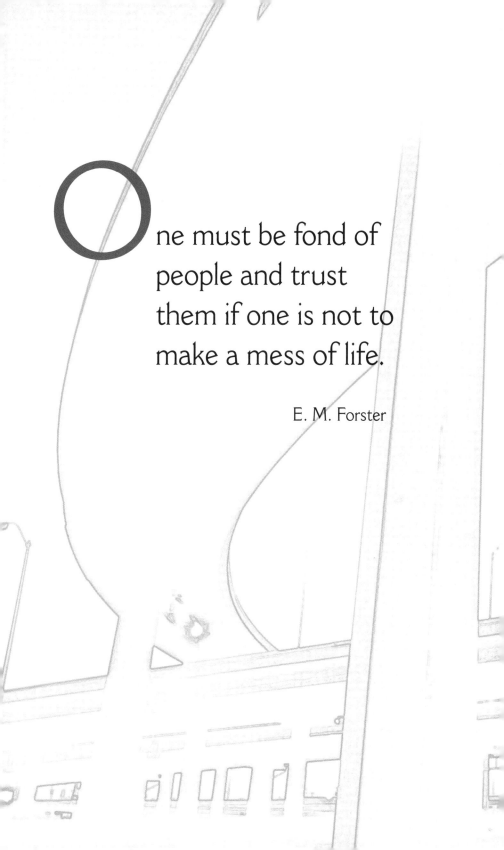

One must be fond of people and trust them if one is not to make a mess of life.

E. M. Forster

"I KNOW YOU'RE THERE — BUT ARE YOU REALLY WORKING?"

Realities and Practicalities of Leading From a Distance

lead (lēd)

1 a: to guide on a way especially by going in advance b: to direct on a course or in a direction

Where Is the Virtual Workplace?

The virtual work world isn't a single, designated "place" – it's actually anywhere that people can and do work. If you manage people you don't see, lead a team that's spread out geographically, or work within a group that is partially remote…then you're part of the virtual workplace. People who aren't in the same location, don't work in the same time zone, or don't see one another face-to-face each day are part of this group. So are telecommuters, "road warriors," geographically dispersed teams, and anyone not located with coworkers.

Even if you work in a more traditional business environment, you're undoubtedly seeing more examples every day of people working virtually. So you'll soon need to apply your leadership skills in this new and changing virtual workplace. Regardless of where people are, when they work, and how often you see them, you need to lead, manage, and motivate for results…from a distance.

The Technology Factor

Technology has allowed the virtual workplace to become a reality. And it plays a key role in helping leaders ensure that the job gets done wherever and whenever people are working. The importance of having the right technology really becomes obvious when things don't go well or fall short of needs and expectations. When the right technology tools are combined with the right skills, the virtual workplace can really "hum" along nicely, making communication and productivity possible.

To communicate in the virtual workplace, you must become competent and confident in the use of technology tools. Of course, being an effective communicator is important for any leader. But as a distance leader, you must "listen to see" – using your ears rather than your eyes for picking up on subtle cues that indicate a problem, concern, or opportunity to provide needed coaching. Think about how easily you facilitate face-to-face meetings; getting as good at leading virtual meetings is your new target.

Another example of using technology to accomplish routine tasks in new ways is the arena of performance management. Whether you're facing a significant performance problem or you merely need to coach a team member for either improvement or success, it's important that you address these situations promptly. Distance can't be an obstacle to identifying problems, talking about concerns, or praising performance. You can't wait for an opportunity to "bump into" a team member to have these discussions. And you can't just wonder if – or hope that – work is getting done. Rather, as a leader of a distributed team, you must use available technology tools for timely problem-solving, coaching, and recognition discussions. Sure – talking about performance issues and coaching for success might feel easier to handle in a face-to-face setting, but the virtual workplace doesn't usually offer this luxury. A live telephone discussion or videoconference is usually the best option for a coaching discussion, while an e-mail with a quick "atta-boy/girl" praising a team member's work might be appropriate.

Whichever option is best for you and the situation,

JUST DO IT!

To be a virtual bridge builder, remember to:

❖ Stay connected with all members on your team, regardless of where they are and where they work.

❖ Use the best available technology tools to communicate with your team.

❖ Handle problem-solving, coaching, and recognition (praising) discussions promptly to get the best results.

When you build
bridges, you can
keep crossing them.

Rick Pitino

"You can count on me."

Building Bridges of Trust

trust (trŭst)

1 a: assured reliance
on the character,
ability, strength, or
truth of someone or
something b: one in
which confidence is
placed

The cornerstone of every successful working relationship is trust. Without it, you typically end up with unpleasant business environments, disgruntled employees, frustrated customers, and less profitable organizations.

To be sure, building and maintaining trust is no easy task in traditional settings. But it's even *more* challenging for virtual workplaces. Distance, along with the absence of day-to-day interaction, can strain relationships and accelerate the pace at which trust is undermined. So, as a leader in the virtual workplace, fostering trust in relationships with your team, your colleagues, and your boss must be a top priority.

You can build trust by focusing on these key elements of successful relationships: reliability, integrity, and familiarity.

Reliability

Reliability means people have confidence that you will honor the commitments you make. You can't just tell people you're reliable; you have to demonstrate it consistently over time. A good rule of thumb here: under-commit and over-deliver. Don't make a promise on your voice mail greeting to return calls by the end of the day if you can't be certain you will. If you commit to attend on-site meetings or participate in conference calls, show up. People who are remote from you can begin to wonder if you care about them and their concerns when you don't follow through on your promises. While most team members understand the demands and necessary schedule changes you run into as a leader, they still want (and need) your attention and involvement. If your track record for honoring commitments is seen as unreliable, people will have a hard time trusting you.

RELIABILITY TRUST BUILDERS

You can strengthen your reliability in working with your team members and build trust within your team by:

❖ **Keeping a written list** of all the agreements/ promises/commitments you make. Check it frequently.

❖ **Asking your people** to tell you one thing you can do to be more reliable in their eyes — then DO IT!

❖ **Being available** to support and respond to team members. When not available, follow up as soon as possible.

Integrity

Leadership integrity is vital to maintaining trust within your team. Integrity reflects how people perceive your honesty and the degree to which you respect the rights of others. While there's room for plenty of confusion, indirectness, and hidden agendas in work relationships, it's important that you avoid these negative dynamics especially in leading virtually. Without frequent face-to-face opportunities to discuss situations and share concerns, perceptions can become exaggerated and emotions can run high.

INTEGRITY TRUST BUILDERS

Demonstrate integrity in your day-to-day interactions by:

* **Being honest** in everything you do. Once your honesty as a leader is compromised, trust is lost.

* **Being truthful and forthright** (without being obnoxious about it). People need your honest feedback and want to know what you think. Providing feedback that's balanced and fair will strengthen trust in you as a leader.

* **Avoiding sarcasm, joking, and teasing** in your distance interactions. As a leader, anything "edgy" you say on voice mail, send via e-mail, or blurt out in a conference call can be misinterpreted without you ever having the chance to know, respond, or recover.

* **Maintaining confidences.** Don't allow yourself to be a spreader of gossip or a sharer of confidential information people have entrusted to you.

* **Handling sensitive material appropriately.** Make sure that information meant for your eyes (or ears) only remains confidential.

Familiarity

You've heard the old adage: "Familiarity breeds contempt." The truth is – familiarity breeds trust. But this doesn't just happen; it requires effort.

Research on virtual teams indicates that familiarity is a major contributor to building coworker trust. It's important for people to know one another as *people*. In other words, you need to relate to team members on a personal level – and vice versa. They need to know you as a human being as well.

FAMILIARITY TRUST BUILDERS

You can strengthen relationships and build familiarity with your team members by:

❖ **Talking with them** regularly by telephone.

❖ **Scheduling face-to-face meetings** periodically, whenever possible.

❖ **Using every available minute** when you're visiting on-site offices to see and talk with team members. These face-to-face connections are important in bridging the distance when people are not colocated.

❖ **Attending social events** (retirement parties, baby showers, promotion celebrations), even if that means joining "virtually" by teleconference or videoconference. It's often these little things that humanize you as a leader and strengthen both familiarity and trust.

Continued on next page

FAMILIARITY TRUST BUILDERS (CONTINUED)

❖ **Using all available technology** (e-mail, fax, voice mail, telephone, web conferences, videoconferencing, instant messaging) to stay connected and "visible" within your team.

❖ **Taking time to talk about nonwork matters** whenever appropriate, both asking about and sharing information on topics such as families, hobbies, personal interests, etc.

❖ **Making a point to remember** birthdays and acknowledge special accomplishments of your team members and associates.

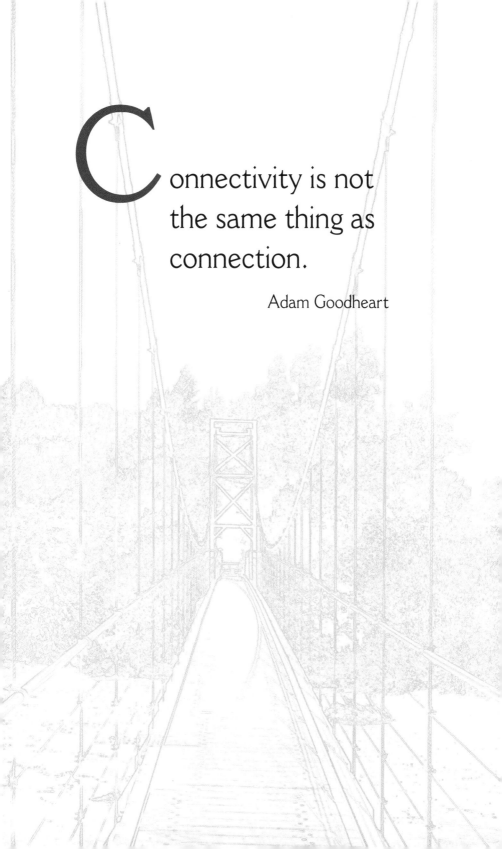

Connectivity is not the same thing as connection.

Adam Goodheart

"Do you see what I hear?"

Building Bridges of Effective Communication

communication
(kə-myü'-ni-kā'shən)

1 a: the exchange of thoughts, messages, or information, as by speech, signals, writing, or behavior

There's no debate – clear, timely, and frequent communication is vital to bridging distances in the virtual workplace. You have a range of options available – "real time" tools and others that can be employed at different times – as needs and circumstances dictate.

Choosing the right way to communicate depends on the situation. Discussing a performance problem, for example, is best handled in a "live" discussion, while using e-mail to distribute meeting notes to team members makes sense.

How often is "enough" when communicating with remote team members? Well, that depends – both on their needs and the type of information you're sharing. But here's the point – even if you communicate facts and data clearly and are right on time with the information, it might not be enough. What's "enough" is really a matter of the *quality* of your communication, not just the quantity. Beyond messages and information about *tasks*, be sure to focus on the *relationship* aspects of what and how you communicate. Create opportunities for people to connect with you in ways they can be heard, feel understood, and know that they're supported.

Have you noticed the absence of "water cooler" conversations in the virtual workplace? These informal ways of talking and sharing information in the traditional workplace need to be replaced in the virtual environment. You can do this by using available technology tools – telephone, instant message, text message, e-mail – to "be present" with an appropriate quantity of "virtual water cooler" chats.

"Distance Dialog"

Good news! – all the things you know about effective communication in a face-to-face interaction still apply in the virtual workplace. What's different is what you *see* vs. what you *hear*. In virtual communication – or "distance dialog" – you lose some of the communication subtleties gleaned from eye contact, body posture, gestures, and voice tone. However, you can overcome this barrier by following a few guidelines:

• Establish the purpose and importance up front.

Sometimes, especially if people are distant from one another, different needs, agendas, concerns, or problems can create multiple expectations. To avoid this obstacle, everyone needs to be clear about why the discussion is taking place *and* why it is important.

• LISTEN!

Out of a desire to be efficient in conveying information, sharing concerns, or establishing expectations, it's easy to overlook the need to listen. Some distance communication tools (such as teleconferencing or other technologies that don't include a visual element) present obstacles to open, interactive communication. For example, in a face-to-face meeting you may notice someone's confusion or desire to make a comment by his or her wrinkled brow – a cue not observable on a teleconference. It's important for you to be aware of the absence of visual cues in virtual meetings and to "reach out" verbally by asking for input, suggestions, or questions. Listen to what is said…and what ISN'T said!

• Avoid monologues.

The tendency to "tell" can be exaggerated by the technology being used and the reluctance of dispersed participants to speak up as readily as they would in a face-to-face discussion. Therefore, you'll need to carefully avoid the "monologue trap" by clearly and frequently inviting interaction and input by others. Sometimes you need to make a report or present information without interruption. In that case, let people know you'll provide time for questions and discussion at the end of your comments.

• Summarize often and confirm understanding.

This gives you the opportunity to review what's been discussed and decided. You can also clear up any misunderstandings in the moment. Do this periodically throughout a virtual interaction, and also at the end.

• Agree on actions/follow-up.

A specific effort to confirm agreements and follow-up activities helps you avoid confusion about who's doing what by when. Depending upon the nature of the interaction, the time urgency, and the complexity of the situation, it may be helpful to also follow up with a summary of actions by memo or e-mail. We all know how easy it is to forget what we discussed with someone; so having a written record can save time and frustration in the future.

Virtual Meetings

"Distance Dialog" guidelines are also important tools for virtual meetings. Along with using these guidelines, consider the various technology options available for your use in meeting with team members. Sometimes you'll need to combine different technologies to have the most productive meeting.

Virtual meetings also involve other factors, like how people will access the meeting and the type of information being shared. Survey participants to determine the best option – use videoconferencing if seeing is important, select teleconferencing if voice-to-voice is sufficient, combine Internet conferencing (for graphics) with a conference call (for audio), etc. Also be aware that introducing participants to technology for meetings may require some training on technical details, procedural issues, or basic etiquette for being courteous, offering input, and asking questions. Once people are comfortable with the technology and their ability to use it, your virtual meetings will be more productive and pleasant for everyone.

Use the following checklist to plan, conduct, and follow up on meetings for dispersed groups:

VIRTUAL MEETING CHECKLIST

Before the meeting:

❏ Plan the **agenda.**

❏ **Distribute** the agenda and information in advance; confirm receipt.

❏ Clarify **responsibilities** (for note taking, timekeeping, meeting leadership, technical support).

❏ **Identify** the appropriate/desired technology to be used. Confirm the availability/accessibility of the selected technology for all participants.

❏ Arrange for **required equipment, information, and people** to be involved.

❏ **Test** the technology. Make sure that things work ahead of time so you can minimize wasting people's time with techno-glitches.

During the meeting:

❏ Encourage all participants to **introduce** themselves (or verbally "sign in") at the beginning of the meeting and **identify** themselves whenever they speak (except for video/net conferencing or well-established teams whose voices are recognized by everyone).

- ❏ Establish **expectations for involvement** by all participants (periodically pause to summarize and ask for questions, discussion, clarification).

- ❏ Ensure that **visual or graphic resources** can be distributed "real-time" or in advance to everyone (via e-mail, fax, Internet, etc.).

- ❏ Remind everyone to **speak slowly, clearly, and in the direction of microphones** or speakerphones, and to request that something be repeated if not heard clearly.

- ❏ Suggest that participants use the **"Mute" button** on their phones to eliminate background noise that might be disruptive to a virtual meeting.

- ❏ Keep to the **schedule.**

After the meeting:

- ❏ Distribute the **meeting summary** in a timely manner, with details regarding agreements and follow-up actions.

- ❏ Schedule any **follow-up meetings** needed.

- ❏ Implement any **action steps** that were agreed to during the meeting.

- ❏ Solicit **feedback** from participants on how similar "meetings" in the future can be enhanced/improved.

Shaping Your E-Communication Culture

Wherever there are people working from afar, leaders must take the initiative to clearly articulate an "e-communication culture." This is done by raising awareness and increasing sensitivity to the communication needs of everyone on the team – and ensuring that all team members understand the impact on their communication methods and techniques. Therefore, it's important to use technology tools that are easily accessible to remote members of the team, regardless of the location or time zone in which they work.

Back in the old days of the traditional workplace, we created standards for document length and "While You Were Out" message slips (remember those?!). The virtual workplace has different needs that must be addressed. So it's important to have a defined set of expectations on the use of various information and communication tools. Beyond your own communication practices, you must also be sure that members of your team are utilizing the best techniques and meeting expectations. You and your virtual team members can use the following *E-Communication Assessment* to evaluate the state of your "e-communication culture" and establish guidelines and agreements for effective communication within your team. That way, all team members will know the "rules of the road;" they'll understand what's expected of them, and what they can expect from others.

E-Communication Assessment

❑ Will e-mail be used for routine communication, while voice mail is the standard for more urgent communication?

❑ When is it appropriate to page people?

❑ What constitutes an acceptable use of cell phones?

❑ What is the appropriate use of PDAs (personal digital assistants) and other wireless devices during meetings?

❑ How should instant messaging be utilized and what limits should be placed on its use?

❑ What types of information should be communicated by voice mail?

❑ What are standards for length of voice mail and e-mail messages and for distribution (who should/should not be copied)?

❑ Are there size limits on documents attached to e-mail?

❑ When should spreadsheets, slide presentations, and multimedia resources be used to share information?

❑ When should the intranet, shared drives, or file transfer sites be used?

❑ What are appropriate methods for filtering information and messages?

❑ How often are associates expected to access various message and information sources?

"SO, WHAT HAVE YOU DONE FOR ME TODAY?"

Building Bridges of Performance

performance

(pər-forˈməns)

1 a: the execution of an action b: something accomplished

The Leader as Performance Manager

The virtual work environment provides unique performance management challenges. Addressing these proactively will have a positive impact on productivity, morale, and results. At the same time, the virtual workplace offers some distinct advantages to the performance management and evaluation process.

Gone are the days of "face time" and the perceived sense that you know they're working because you can see them sitting at their desk or workstation. In reality, the way you know that someone is working – and doing the *right* things the *right* way – is to have clear outcomes. In other words, you don't really know that work is getting done unless you know what's expected, how it's to be done, and how it will be measured. This is where the virtual workplace has a positive impact on your need to manage performance effectively by requiring that clear expectations, behaviors, and measures be defined.

When team members work remotely, you can't totally control how they do their jobs, but you still need to manage their overall performance and results. It can be difficult – for leaders and employees – to discuss performance issues from a distance. Having a clear process with specific steps provides a guide and keeps everyone on track.

Most organizations have implemented some sort of performance management system, with varying degrees of complexity and utility. If there isn't one or isn't an effective one, take the initiative – create your own performance management process that incorporates the basic steps of **goal setting**, **tracking**, and **review**. Or if a system exists but its use isn't reinforced, take the lead and use it within your team. The following guidelines will help you get started:

1. Review the performance management process.

2. Answer questions regarding the process.

3. Discuss organization and department mission/goals.

4. Establish performance goals/expectations.

5. Discuss individual/team/organization needs.

6. Review support/development needs.

7. Establish time frames and dates for future review and follow-up sessions.

8. Offer support for any needed coaching or assistance.

The Leader as Performance Coach

A significant part of your job as a manager and leader is to coach team members. You have coaching discussions that involve addressing performance problems and correcting performance shortfalls. These discussions are usually initiated by you, sometimes follow previous discussions regarding the performance concerns, and typically involve finding ways to correct an unacceptable situation. Many of our models and experiences of coaching have a distinctly face-to-face dimension – think about when you've been coached in sports, by teachers, and by managers. We have less hands-on experience with distance coaching, and this presents some unique challenges for virtual leaders.

An important opportunity to coach employees occurs when you set goals and regularly review results. In a remote work environment, your need to manage the performance process remains unchanged. What changes is your use of technology tools for communicating throughout the process, including alternatives to face-to-face meetings.

You'll also have discussions with employees that involve coaching for success. In these situations, you and the employee will work together to decrease the possibility of performance problems later. Either you or the team member, who may make a specific request for your help, can initiate these discussions. You can incorporate coaching-for-success discussions when conducting new employee orientations, delegating new assignments, preparing a client response, or creating a new project team. And all of these situations can be handled from a distance.

When face-to-face discussions aren't possible, shoot for "voice-to-voice" meetings for coaching. Use the telephone as a primary way of connecting "live" and supplement with other technology tools like e-mail and other online conferencing techniques to share documents and reports.

The following coaching discussion guidelines will help you plan and conduct distance-coaching discussions.

COACHING DISCUSSION GUIDLINES

1. Clarify the purpose and desired outcomes of the discussion.
   Why are we "meeting" and what needs to be accomplished?

2. Review information you have and ask for additional information and ideas.
   Discuss available data, welcome input on additional data, suggestions, obstacles, opportunities.

3. Establish or review objectives.
   Communicate outcomes, goals, timelines.

4. Discuss ideas and concerns.
   Encourage sharing of issues, problems, obstacles, suggestions, solutions.

5. Agree on goals or plan of action.
   Confirm WHAT will be done, HOW it will be done, and by WHEN; clarify any needs for additional support.

6. Set follow-up.
   Agree on review/follow-up dates.

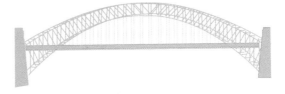

SUMMARY

Many techniques for leading in the virtual workplace are similar to traditional leadership methods. Key competencies, such as communication, goal setting, coaching, team building, performance management, etc., don't change as your team becomes more dispersed. However, the ways in which these leadership skills are applied is changing as more teams become virtual and more people work remotely from one another and from you.

As a leader in this increasingly virtual world, you are helping to build new bridges to success by strengthening trust, communicating effectively, and achieving results. Preparing yourself and your team for the virtual workplace is key to your continued effectiveness as a leader – not just down the road, but RIGHT NOW!

The virtual workplace is not a phenomenon of the future, but a reality for leaders today.

And like other changes of this magnitude, there's little chance that we're going back to the way things used to be.

So, become a bridge builder – and lead the way into the new virtual workplace!

ABOUT THE AUTHOR

 **Debra A. Dinnocenzo** is president of VirtualWorks!, (www.VirtualWorksWell.com) which provides training and resources for people in the virtual workplace. The firm specializes in telework, virtual teams, and work-life balance and helps people lead more productive and balanced lives.

A seasoned senior executive and experienced virtual leader with more than two decades of corporate and academic experience, Dinnocenzo has an extensive background in human resources sales and marketing. A dynamic speaker, consultant, and author, she is a nationally recognized expert in the field of telework and a frequent speaker at national conferences on virtual workplace and work-life balance issues. She is often quoted in the media and is widely published on virtual work strategies and techniques. Dinnocenzo is the author of *101 Tips for Telecommuters* and coauthor of *Dot Calm: The Search for Sanity in a Wired World*.

An active member of her community and industry, Dinnocenzo serves on numerous boards, including the Telework Coalition; AAA (American Automobile Association); University of Pittsburgh Medical Center Passavant Hospital; and Passavant Hospital Foundation.

Dinnocenzo holds Bachelor of Science and Masters of Arts degrees in Management from Central Michigan University. She holds an adjunct faculty position with Duquesne University where she teaches an online graduate course, *Leadership in the Virtual Workplace*. Additionally, she serves on the faculty of the Institute for Management Studies.

ABOUT THE PUBLISHER

Since 1977, The WALK THE TALK® Company has helped organizations, worldwide, achieve success through Ethical Leadership and Values-Based Business Practices. And we're ready to do the same for you!

We offer a full range of proven resources and customized services – all designed to help you turn shared values like *Integrity, Respect, Responsibility, Customer Service, Trust,* and *Commitment* into workplace realities.

To order additional copies of this high-impact resource, contact
The WALK THE TALK® Company at 888.822.9255 or visit:

www.walkthetalk.com

You will discover our full range of products and services to include:

◆ "How-To" Handbooks and Support Material

◆ Video Training Programs

◆ Corporate Gift Books

◆ Do-It-Yourself Training Resources

◆ Keynotes and Conference Presentations

◆ The popular ***Santa's Leadership Secrets*** and ***Start Right… Stay Right*** product lines

◆ 360° Feedback Processes

and much more!

Also consider these other powerful
WALK THE TALK® Resources!

The Manager's Communication Handbook
This powerful handbook will allow you to connect with employees and create understanding, support, and acceptance crucial to your individual and organizational success. $9.95

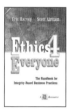

Ethics4Everyone
Unique and powerful resource for employees at ALL levels. It provides practical information to guide individual actions, decisions, and daily behaviors. When it comes to ethics, everyone is responsible…everything counts! $9.95

180 Ways To Walk The Recognition Talk
A powerful guide packed with ideas and suggestions for reinforcing good performance and creating a culture of appreciation. $9.95

Walking The Talk Together
Focusing on shared responsibility, this easy-to-read handbook pinpoints the ten critical behaviors that everyone must adopt in order to build a team-oriented environment of trust, commitment, and integrity. $9.95

Positive Discipline
Practical time-tested techniques for resolving performance problems quickly and permanently…while strengthening employee commitment in the process. $9.95

ORDER FORM

Have questions? Need assistance? Call 1.888.822.9255

 Please send me additional copies of HOW TO LEAD FROM A DISTANCE

1-99 copies: $9.95 ea.   100-499 copies: $8.95 ea.   500+ copies: call *1.888.822.9255*

HOW TO LEAD FROM A DISTANCE
Building Bridges in the Virtual Workplace ____copies   X $_____   = $_____

Additional Books From WALK THE TALK

The Manager's Communication Handbook	____copies	X $ 9.95	= $_____
Ethics4Everyone	____copies	X $ 9.95	= $_____
180 Ways To Walk The Recognition Talk	____copies	X $ 9.95	= $_____
Walking The Talk Together	____copies	X $ 9.95	= $_____
Positive Discipline	____copies	X $ 9.95	= $_____

Product Total	$_____
*Shipping & Handling	$_____
Subtotal	$_____
Sales Tax:	
TX Sales Tax – 8.25%	$_____
CA Sales/Use Tax	$_____
TOTAL (U.S. Dollars Only)	$_____

(Sales & Use Tax Collected on TX & CA Customers Only)

*Shipping and Handling Charges

No. of Items	1-4	5-9	10-24	25-49	50-99	100-199	200+
Total Shipping	$6.75	$10.95	$17.95	$26.95	$48.95	$84.95	$89.95+$0.25/book

Call 972.243.8863 for quote if outside continental U.S. Orders are shipped ground delivery 3-5 business days.
Next and 2nd business day delivery available – call 1.888.822.9255.

Name_____ Title _____

Organization _____

Shipping Address _____
_{No P.O. Boxes}

City_____ State____ Zip _____

Phone _____ Fax _____

E-Mail_____

Charge Your Order: ❑ MasterCard   ❑ Visa   ❑ American Express

Credit Card Number_____ Exp. _____

❑ Check Enclosed (Payable to: The WALK THE TALK Company)

❑ Please Invoice (Orders over $250 ONLY) P.O. # (required)_____

Prices effective March, 2006 are subject to change.

PHONE
1.888.822.9255
or 972.243.8863
M-F, 8:30 – 5:00 Central

FAX
972.243.0815

ONLINE
www.walkthetalk.com

MAIL
WALK THE TALK CO.
2925 LBJ Fwy, #201
Dallas, TX 75234